WALK A WHILE
IN MY SHOES

WALK A WHILE IN MY SHOES

ROB ABDUL

To order additional copies of this book, contact:
Xlibris Corporation
0-800-644-6988
www.xlibrispublishing.co.uk
Orders@xlibrispublishing.co.uk
302875

CONTENTS

QUATRAINS

DEDICATION

I dedicate this book to the love of my life Nicky Kaler; my God-gifted soul mate. She is always there for me, like a lighthouse in the storm of life, lighting my path, guiding me, protecting me, being my gyroscope, keeping me focused and loving me like no other. I am so blessed. Any success of mine I attribute to you my Goddess.

For the miracle that is life, may God bless my brothers Razzak, and Kalam (my baby brother) and my Father, Jamal Ahmed who are with God in his kingdom now.

You are all greatly missed and loved.

ACKNOWLEDGMENTS

I have many wonderful people in my life that I offer heartfelt gratitude and appreciation for playing their part in making this book possible:

Nicky Kaler, my Nicky, thank you for being a poet's muse. My muse.

Mark Whittingham, the most skilled wordsmith I have ever come across. Thank you for your help and advice I am forever indebted to you my friend.

Lisa Lynch, thank you for the late hours and for taking the time to proof read my work. You are a dear friend to Nicky and I.

David Hunter, thank you for making my idea for a picture come true.

Paul Whitehouse, Managing Director of Whitehouse Mainwaring, for being my teacher, mentoring me, and always reminding me to leave a legacy behind. This book is a small step in that direction.

Angi Egan, who gave me an abundance of advice that got me started.

The wonderful team at Xlibris publishing, namely Naomi Orleans for the guidance and support you have provided me.

Paul Kaler, my father-in-law, for always making me aim for the stars when my destination was just the moon.

I thank all my loved ones for their unwavering faith, criticism and endless love. You all know who you are. I carry you all safely in my heart.

My wonderful Mother without whom I would never have existed. Thank-you.

PREFACE

Walk a While in My Shoes is a collection of poems that are an account of one man's journey in life, from a teenager right into adulthood.

It is a record of the key events and moments through hurt, frustration and at times, sheer inspiration, that compelled me to write my poetry.

In essence, the central themes of this collection of works are love, loss and an admiration of femininity.

The journey starts when I am at the tender age of fifteen years old. The background setting is the back streets of Birmingham, Middle England in the mid 1990s. Originating from a large family of two sisters and six brothers, I was a middle child. In my teens, not being heard or noticed was the reason poetry became an escape to vent my bottled up emotions that ran riot, in verse form on a page.

My parents were going through a separation whilst I was is in the final year of high school. It was then that a poem I had written in my creative writing class was entered for a competition. This marked the beginning of my writing adventure.

The adventure has had its highs and lows. The lowest of which was the loss of my brother Kalam in a tragic road accident. The never ending high point started when I was twenty two years old. That is when I met the love of my life. As it was true for Romeo and Juliet, who each came from opposing households, the same was true for Nicky and her Rob.

Nicky comes from a Sikh family and I from a Muslim family. These are two religious backgrounds that conventionally do not mix. This struggle gave access to a whole new reservoir of inspiration to tap into.

TEENAGE YEARS

PERFECTION OF BEAUTY

Thee has the combination of all the qualities that delight the senses and
pleases ones mind,
You are a very attractive and well formed woman,
Thy possesses the beauty spot,
A small dark coloured patch worn on thy face to mark an adornment,
As foil to your complexion.

Is the beauty I see in thee,
Or in my eyeful eyes?
Admirably admirable to have the honour to view a glance and gaze a very
Beauty and attractive sight of thee.

How long did the one of class of spiritual beings that attendant upon God,
Take to make thee?

Thou always admissible to bind your heart with mine,
Are you amongst the finest beauty to ever walk this planet?

Let us happily examine thy beauty and give grace into,
Those looks that set fire to a man's heart!
From whom an hour,
Brings a lover in thy shadow.

Lovers thy have to comfort and despair,
Which like spirits do suggest thee,
The better spirit is a man right.

POWER OF LOVE

A woman's heart is a battery,
Which is charged with love and affection.

When a man breaks her dear heart,
She is left overwhelmed by grief and disappointment.

A man's heart is a rechargeable battery,
Which is charged with lies, deceit and deception.

When a woman breaks his heart,
He is not overwhelmed by grief and disappointment,
He does not need to haul through his life to live,
All he does is recharge.

LIFE

O you, one who dares devour life,
In what order in what strife,
Why you deny faith in religion,
Causing conflict and causing collision,
Why self-inflict ruin on your soul,
Why open the gateway to hell, why open a hole.
Life is life in any angle,
Whatever it be pleasuring or in a tangle,
The God descended man and woman to create Heaven on Earth,
O no, not to say death after birth!

MIRAGE

You started to heal me,
You made me forget my pain,
In my desert you brought rain,
With that rain came hope,
With that hope came faith,
With faith came love true love,
Sweet summer has returned.

WHEN MY HEART DIED

When my heart died,
I could not live for much longer,
My broken heart and its hunger,
I could no longer hold onto reality.
With my heart in such pain and calamity,
Now I cannot say if I am dead or alive,
I just exist where time does not survive.

MIRACLE

The first miracle was when we first met,
The second was when we first kissed,
The third came when we fell in love,
The fourth my sweet love,
The fourth miracle is on its way . . .

DIVINE INSPIRATION

Retire fair sun beneath the celestial horizon,
For thy civil days duty for now has been fulfilled,
Fall gracefully and endure my earnest moon to arise,
As she ascends above the airy region so elegantly,
The tree tops marvel at the luxurious silver kiss.
The exquisite sight of her vestal livery offers,
Enticing bounty to the envious tides.

By her virtuous divine light the scene is a brilliant fairyland,
Unveiling nature's integrity of magnificence and splendour,
Where she uses her delicate limbs to move through the air,
As a slight gust of wind blows her hair from her face,
The comeliness I contemplate is of exceptional grace,
Her eyes glance and connote every thought in my heart,
As she ascends above the land she glows brighter than a star,
She fills the land with her divine luminescence and departs to her home.

Now we do not meet, we live apart,
Memories of her are now rationed in my heart,
'Tis dusk, night's cloak which embraces my soul,
'Tis dusk, night's cloak which does not console,
O mother of darkness, father of flame,
Perish my soul if I am to blame.

DREAMING IN A DREAM

At my own pace and sweet will,
Did my soul convince my heart for the very first kill,
In at the kill I was to propose to her for a date,
My heart it did tremble with fear and fate,
Was I to rest my heart's cry hanging on the sharpest end of time?
My heart it would not agree, and refused to undergo through any more crime!
With this horrifying thought the day turned so blue that it was suddenly a
dreadful night . . .

A blue moon rose which gave my eyes a tender fright,
I felt as though Love had tied me firmly to the cold ground,
Now only she and I seemed to be the two lonely souls around.

No sound was then proposed to be heard,
Though my eyesight not focused but blurred,
I could see her in the distant mist of the dark night,
She roams the landscape under the virgin light,
The Love birds sing their own song,
And constantly remind me that I am not wrong.

She decided to approach me with a smile and in a very slick fashion,
Right away my heart granted love and so much passion,
As she approached me the night was turning into day,
The place had changed and we were in a sweet bay,
The shine of the star lit her face,
The beauty my eyes lived to see was so great,
That my mind could not work out why I left it so late,
With one touch of her lips,
My mind extinguished all emotions tense,
Then Love decided to run around us and build a heart shaped fence.

OUT OF LOVE

And in this desert that is life,
If you haven't lost in love,
Then you haven't lived to die,
And there is a fire burning inside me,
And hope has turned to ashes,
And purpose,
Purpose is the oasis I need to find,
Faith is the oasis I need to hold onto,
I am stronger,
And it takes a stronger person to cry,
And when the angels come to take me home,
I shall embrace the light. I will not resist.

WIDOW

The curtains haven't been drawn for weeks,
Darkness lights the entire room,
She is lying on her bed,
She takes her last few breaths.
Her heart beats rhythmically,
Slowly turning her white gown to red,
As memories seep into her head,
Tears start to roll down her face.

TWENTIES AND BEYOND

YOU ARE SO SPECIAL

Finding true love is like,
Finding a single grain of sand,
From billions upon,
Billions of grains of sand,
On the entire world's,
Beaches put together.

I waited 22 years before I was,
Blessed with my diamond,
My eyes saw for the first time,
My heart beat thereafter,
With a sole purpose.
I had found my sphere of destiny.

EYES

I have never seen eyes,
Eyes as exquisite as yours,
Eyes as deep and intense,
Eyes that caress the soul,
Eyes that pierce the soul,
Eyes that generously glance,
Like a pair of binary stars,
They shower their light,
Upon their captivating subjects,
Upon a delightful planet,
Sustaining all life on that planet,
My planet my heart,
Bathes in your endless rays,
Glances from your eyes,
Speak of such holy rhetoric,
Without ever speaking a word,
I try to decipher your rays,
But I am overwhelmed,
When I look at your eyes,
I want to set sail for the stars.

LADY LOVE

Heaven is not heaven if You are not there,
Your presence is of heavenly presence,
You ignite the very air around your flare,
One is drawn to your warmth, your ambience.

Even a blind man shall speak of your exquisiteness,
It is not limited to vision, it is also felt with liberation,
And if one was unfortunate enough to not witness You,
With sight or hearing, he shall express,
Your healing touch that soothes and comforts.

Bless Heavenly Father for I have eyes and I can see,
Beauty that you bestow with immeasurable measure,
Your eyes are like two diamonds, the gateway to my soul,
Your lips too sacred to kiss but to marvel at,
Each strand of your hair exhibits radiance.

Bless Heavenly Father for I have been liberated,
I am in love with Lady Love.

DESCRIBING MY LOVE FOR YOU

Describing my love for you
Is like trying to describe how an Angel flies,
I can tell you that this Angel has wings,
His feathers are vibrant white and silky smooth,
He is your Knight in shining amour,
The "one" you've dreamt of,
Since you were a little girl,
He understands you not just by listening to you,
He understands by feeling your feelings.
His touch heals,
His kiss redeems your soul.

In God's Kingdom he is your companion.
Beside him you sit, without him you are incomplete,
How he musters flight is simply magic,
When God exhales, God's breath causes lift to those wings,
You are this Angel's heart and the only prevailing thought on this Angel's mind.

Together we are the Pinnacle of God's creation.
That creation is "true love"—even God's heart melts,
When he sees what he has sown has grown into you and I,
That is how my love is for you,
Divine and magic,
I love you,
Powered by God the Almighty,
Moses, Jesus, Mohammed, Guru Nanak, Buddha, Bhagwan . . .

MY GODDESS

When God commissioned,
You to be made,
Heaven and all its Angels,
Were given three days,
To rest, reflect and rejoice,
For what they had created,
Even God had a lump,
In his throat when he saw,
His angels' labour of love,
You set a precedence,
In Heaven "my love".

CIVIL WAR

My troops have all put up their white flags,
You have their unconditional surrender,
Wounded and sick they are all on their knees,
They concede your totalitarian government.

And yet the sound of sirens hail,
Yet another wave of incoming attack,
A blitzkrieg of aerial bombardment,
Pilots that never miss their targets.

Fire and billowing smoke from earlier attacks,
Has decimated the land and blackened the sky,
I cannot advance or retreat, attack or defend,
Forgive me, my love, have mercy, ceasefire.

BROKEN PROMISE

I have fallen from grace,
I can no longer show you my face,
I did what I said I would never do,
Broke your heart and made you blue.

I did not set out to hurt you,
My crime is that I did not think it through,
And that I kept things from you,
I know now that I should have told you.

I know you need time to heal,
To accept the truth as real,
I know you said you forgive me,
But I do not forgive me.

I lost your trust and cannot get it back,
O how I dream of redemption,
Of the day you trust me once more,
I know that day will never come,
And it is all because of my own doing.

I fantasise about only having minutes to live,
And taking my last breath in your arms,
If you would afford me the grace,
I want to make a dying declaration to you?
I heard a dying person never lies,
Neither would I my love,
You will have to trust me this one last time.

I want to say:
I did not set out to hurt you,
I know now that I should have told you,
I am sorry from the pit of my soul,
I protected you from all else but myself,
Next life I will not hurt you,
You were the reason I was sent to Earth,
You are the love of my life.

MEAGRE EXISTENCE

Ever since I broke your heart,
I am realising the gravity of my actions,
I am not sure if I have fallen,
Fallen asleep or awoken to a different reality.

During the mornings you are not next to me,
I feel devastated for a few brief moments,
Until the memory returns of what I have done,
A tall tale of lies and deceit that I have spun.

The days are so cold,
So cold without you,
Even the Sun hides from me,
But occasionally the clouds break.

The sun has no choice but to show herself,
I see her with baited breath,
I do not feel her heat, she denies me that,
I can only attempt to compensate,
With many extra layers of clothing.

Maybe a walk in the park,
Will clear my head,
But sitting on a park bench,
I realise that the birds,
No longer sing their tune to me.

When night falls there are no stars,
No stars to guide me home,
In my dreams all I see is days gone by,
I wish I never awake from them.

LOVE IS SACRIFICE

To give up your love within a moment's notice,
To feel all and not utter a word to anyone,
To busy yourself and still think of your Love,
To smile while a storm ravages you from inside,
To give up your seat in Heaven and happily enter Hell,
To give up without thinking twice,
True love, my Love, is sacrifice.

SYMPHONY OF LOVE

In your heart there is a radio,
Simply turning it on is not enough,
If you have found your soul mate,
They will help you tune your radio set,
So you can receive the symphony of Love,
The only other way is if you've found God.
If you are fortunate to have found both in this life,
Your radio will not only receive but transmit too,
The message of love, oneness and tranquillity.

THE THINKER

My first memory of you was,
When we were playing in the garden,
I told you all my secrets,
You knew everything,
Even that which I hadn't spoken of,
When I had no one,
I had you my Love.

Every time I cried,
You consoled me,
Whenever I cried myself to sleep,
You lay next to me,
Uttering wise words to me,
You were my friend,
When I had none,
You taught me to look inside,
That true love starts from within,
I never doubted you my Love,
You were my first love,
I still sing your praises,
We have come so far together,

And yet every time I look in the mirror,
I see your face my Love and still do not recognise,
I still am learning who you really are.

FATHER

When I,
Cannot see,
In the fog,
Of war,
I charge ahead,
As our Father,
My father,
In Heaven,
Sees all,
Knows all,
His angels,
Clear my path,
Guiding me,
Protecting me.

RETURNING THE GIFT

I held you as a baby,
You were so tiny your eyes still closed,
I felt your heart beat, it was racing,
You were the cutest thing I ever saw.

Through the years as we grew,
We were more like friends than brothers,
We never fought; instead we did fun things,
I could trust and rely on you.

I remember the day I left home,
You tried to talk me out of it.
My mind made up I was having none of it,
I needed to pave my way in this life.

Years passed, you went to university,
You were engaged to be married too,
We saw less and less of each other,
But I was still so happy for you.

I still remember being woken at 6am,
To hear that you were in a car accident,
I was not sure at first if I was dreaming,
At the hospital I realised I was in a nightmare.

Seeing all those wires and tubes,
Made me feel so afraid for you,
Your brain had bled and stopped working,
The doctors said that there was nothing they could do.

Their best estimates were minutes to hours,
Once the machine keeping you alive was switched off,
That was not an easy decision to take,
The switch pressed, I rested my hand on your chest,
I felt your heart beat. It was racing like 22 years before,
You were still the cutest thing I ever saw.

I never got to say goodbye,
You lost consciousness at the accident scene,
I never got to say I love you,
I say it now, I love you,
The night you crossed over I questioned God's angels,
Why didn't they protect you?
Then I realised that they were protecting you,
They had come to shepherd you through the valley of darkness.

GIFT FROM GOD

I waited for you to arrive from the heavens,
Each visit to hospital with our parents,
The heavens never gave,
My wanting heart began to crave.

I always hoped, I prayed for a girl,
Then soon after I began to despair,
Why would God fill my heart with such a desire?
And not fulfil it and leave me on fire?!

And then one day I found you,
Miss Giggles with a storm in her teacup.

Sometimes the desire for something is so strong,
That when God finally delivers you are left speechless.

You are everything that I imagined you to be,
I love you "my" baby sister.

SECOND CHANCE

Staring at a hospital ceiling,
Drawn to the unearthly light,
Delirious from all the drugs,
And taking your last breaths,
You will come to realise,
Realise prevailing thoughts,
Things unsaid or undone,
You thought you had time,
Or pride had tied you down,
Now you see all the time,
Time wasted on all vanity.

You'll want one more chance,
To go back to your body,
Being outside yourself,
Made you see all that was,
Already within you,
What am I to do with you?
I can send you back,
With the following words,
Be true to your heart,
Tomorrow may not come,
Put aside pride and vanity,
Live and love,
Live as if it is your last day.

PRAISE YOU

I have nothing but praise for you,
For your strength, form, and beauty of your kind,
I owe my existence to you,
Your labour of love that you carried for months,
Loved me, nurtured and fed me off your own body.

I have nothing but praise for you,
For your strength, form, and beauty of your kind,
In this uneven world you have fought to be equal,
Against tyranny often by forsaking yourself,
Against a world that would not exist without you,
Against a world that owes its existence to you,
Despite this and all that is done unto your kind,
You still put us before yourself,
You still offer your own body as sustenance to us,
You still care for us,
You still love and protect us.

I have nothing but praise for you,
For your strength, form, and beauty of your kind,
Perhaps our saving grace is that you're kind,
Womankind came from the rib of a man,
Perhaps the virtues that were transferred to you,
We still retain something and we can change,
And if nothing else,
These words will serve testament to you, Woman.

LOVE TRANSCENDS TIME

When I was thirsty I would reach for some water,
That would quench my thirst for a while,
When I was hungry I would eat,
Eating at first was only so that I would stay alive,
Not for me, but for my family and for you my love,
I had to my love, because I could not let the world see,
I was collapsing inside myself with a false smile on my face,
Letting you go had left such a huge void within me,
I wished for death with every baited breath at first,
But life had other ideas for me my love,
I put up no resistance as other lives were involved,
Drifting on life's river I let the fast currents overwhelm me,
Away from your heart into someone else's arms.
Days turned to weeks and weeks turned to years.

I never forgot you my love in all these years,
To be honest I did not try to remember you either,
But I would be always reminded of you,
Birthdays, Valentines, and at Christmas time,
Sometimes I would hear our favourite song on the radio,
Or I would visit places where we would once meet.

Romeo and Juliet died for each other,
They took the easy way out,
We buried our love,
We sacrificed ourselves,
We could not protest,
We could not fight,
Against the wrath of the world,
Through that sacrifice I lost,
A part of my heart to you.

CONVERSATIONS WITH LOVE

I asked Love "what are you my Love?"
He replied,
"I am a butterfly from a foreign sky,
My beauty is for all of nature,
Like the sunlight my essence is for all,
I do not withhold my beauty from the good or the bad,
I know not how to withhold my light,
All I know is how to shine for all my beloved"

You are so beautiful my Love,
I am so mesmerised by your form,
You radiate waves of peace and calm,
I want to hold you Love in my palms,
I need to keep you Love in my palms,
I do not want you to leave me ever,
I fear that I will lose you in this life,
Choose me, please stay with me?

Ever since I stepped into your light,
I feel the glow I see around you inside me now,
I feel my soul resonate at your frequency,
I feel connected to you my Love,
In my heart I have endless fields for you,
The light you gave me cultivated these fields,
These are endless fields for all,
As far as my eyes can see my Love,
I know nothing else now but you my Love,
You are truth that I have been searching for,
That search has ended in me.

Now I realise I am no longer afraid to lose you,
You made me grow and taught me to become you.

GOD GIFTED SOUL MATE

I don't know what year it was,
Maybe a thousand million years ago,
Because I had not mass,
I was a just a latrino particle,
Wandering through the vastness,
Of the known universe,
Alone and without a cause,
Waiting for our lord dear God,
To guide me to you.

Meanwhile I had seen many wonders,
Sunsets in foreign worlds,
Hydrogen gas stirred and turned to stars,
And the same stars die in supernova,
Spawning life with iron dust,
For many millennia I witnessed,
This cycle of life and death repeat,

Until I witnessed you appear from nothing,
Until I saw angel Haniel appear alongside you,
And escort thee my beloved's soul,
Through the vastness of the cosmos,
Your destination was set to Earth,
You were on the outskirts of the Milky Way,
When I felt your existence,
Your soul's light is what I was waiting for,
God alerted me to you for that I'm sure.

Travelling faster than the speed of light,
I raced for Earth before you,
I got here a year and three days before you,
I was born with no memory of you,
It wouldn't be until two more decades,
Until I saw you once more,
And I could gaze into your precious eyes,
And recalled this entire galactic journey,
And then fall in love with you,
You are the reason I was sent to Earth,
You are my Achilles heel and my greatest strength,
Only with you is my destiny.

When it is time for me to depart Earth,
Please find solace in the words,
Should my fate be that I leave before you,
My soul will be waiting as it did before,
Just like the universe our souls became into existence,
We do not die we merely change properties,
From mass on Earth to pure energy as souls.

QUATRAINS

KNIGHT IN SHINING ARMOUR

I am your Knight in shining armour,
I will change your want for me into a need,
I will heal your heart and take you above,
I am your angel, my name is Love.

LOST LOVE

It does not matter what I think,
You have made up your mind,
Heavy-hearted I can only sink,
Only you can save me from the brink.

CONFUSION

Should I turn off emotion inside my head,
Awake my heart and soul if not already dead?
I am pining away for something I will never find,
Maybe you are not a mirage and it is all in my mind?

MY TRUTH

I'm losing, losing blood, my heart it's bleeding,
I've fallen, fallen for you and now you're leaving,
Memories of you will keep my soul alive,
And if living without you is living, then I'd rather die.

CHESS

I know it is illogical for me,
Your king to sacrifice oneself,
For you my queen,
But there is no logic in love.

PRAISE

My heart glows with love and praise for you,
Follows you on your orbit like the Earth does the Sun,
Your gravity attracts us all to you,
Nothing can compare to basking in your light and love.

THE FOUR Cs OF YOU

You are Cut from the finest stardust,
You Care like love at first sight,
You have Charm that cupid learns from,
You are Curvaceous, a delight to any mans eyes.

MOTHER

You carried me for nine months and more,
I owe my existence to your hard work and toil,
I hope that I myself am the recompense for sure,
I will carry you for the rest of your life like a royal.

ABOUT THE AUTHOR

Rob's day job is a far cry from that of a Poet as he is a leading and well renowned figure in the world of Ecommerce. Ever since winning a competition at High School he has nurtured his love and passion for poetry.

Although Rob's work has been published on several occasions, this book celebrates his first collection of completed works. Rob hopes to illustrate his journey through the eyes of his tender teenage years right through into the extraordinary man he is today. Come and walk a while in his shoes.